The Backbone of Leadership

THE
BACKBONE
OF
Leadership

EMBRACING THE RESPONSIBILITY
TO LEAD FROM BEHIND

Foreword by Eric Thomas, PhD (E.T. the Hip-Hop Preacher)
L. DAVID HARRIS

HARRIS
Author Services

The Backbone of Leadership: Embracing the Responsibility to Lead from Behind
Written by L. David Harris

Published by Harris Author Services
30 N Gould Street, Ste 6642
Sheridan, WY 82801

ISBN: 979-8-9878503-7-4

Disclaimer: This book is designed to provide accurate and authoritative information regarding the subject matter covered. It is sold with the understanding that the author and publisher are not engaged in rendering legal, financial, or other professional advice. If expert assistance is required, the services of a competent professional should be sought.

DEDICATION

To my all-time favorite professional support person, Michca-Mae Bonner.

During the most challenging leadership position I have ever held—leading the department of communication in our organization through the COVID-19 crisis—you were the backbone of leadership to me. Under unspeakable pressure from all sides, you stood by me, working tirelessly in the trenches, providing exceptional service and quality work as we served the 108,000+ member constituency in our region.

If every Chief Operating Officer (COO), Chief of Staff, Vice President, General Manager, Senior Director/Manager, Regional Manager/Director, Associate

Director, Assistant/Deputy Director, Program Manager, Team Leader/Supervisor, or anyone in a critical support role adopted your mindset of service, the world would undoubtedly be a better place.

God bless you.

I am forever in your debt.

Contents

ONE MORE DISCLAIMER

If I am your coach or consultant, and what you're reading seems to resemble your situation, it may be coincidental. I value your trust and guide you with complete confidentiality. I would only write or share your details with your explicit, written permission.

One More Disclaimer

FOREWORD

Listen to me closely—when it comes to leadership, a lot of people talk the talk...but very few walk the walk. That's why I'm super excited about this book, and more importantly, what it represents. My brother L. David Harris (we call him L.D.), doesn't just talk about leadership—he lives, eats, breathes, and sleeps it! He understands the grind, the sacrifice, and the commitment it takes to be the Backbone of Leadership.

I learned the hard way that without a team of people making sure your vision becomes a reality, without those backbones of leadership, nothing great can ever happen. I've been a CEO for over 20 years, and I've always had big dreams...but until I got a team to help me execute, they were just that: DREAMS!

That's where this book comes in. L.D. is one of the best in the game at helping secondary leaders like you understand your power and your purpose. In this book and workbook, he's going to walk you through how to support your leader, how to handle pressure when things get tough, how to grow and develop the people around you, and how to be that steady hand that holds the organization together. L.D. isn't going to give you a bunch of theory, then send you on your way—he's giving you the actual tools you need to be a game-changer in your role. He's breaking down the practical strategies, giving you the truth about what it takes to stand strong under pressure, and how to push through when others might buckle.

So, if you're ready to take your leadership to the next level and embrace the fact that you are the backbone of leadership, then you owe it to yourself to go ALL-IN on this book. L.D. isn't going to show you how to just survive in your role, or even how to strive for better – he's going to give you the blueprint to THRIVE. By the end of this book, you'll be able to lead with power and grace, and leave a legacy that people will remember long after the spotlight on the primary leader is gone.

I need you to hear me when I say this: you are invaluable! The work you do is necessary, and this book is going to help you do it at the highest level. I know you're probably not about being in the spotlight—you know that it's about making sure the whole team wins. That's what being the backbone of leadership is all about, and that's what this book will help you do.

Now you know. Let's GO! – Eric Thomas, PhD (E.T. the Hip-Hop Preacher)

Foreword

INTRODUCTION

In 2016, I published a book titled, *Shine: Choosing Success When Failure Seems Inevitable*. In the chapter titled, *Helping Others Become Successful*, I wrote the following, which is the perfect starting point of this book: "I have invested a large portion of my adult life in helping others achieve success. It got so crazy one year that I wondered what I was doing wrong! Every time I helped someone achieve their goals, even those who had identical goals to mine, they were more successful than I. I could not figure out how they simply employed the steps and principles I would give them and they would inevitably surpass my level of success (or so I thought).

Then it hit me: My purpose is to help others become successful. For me, that is success! It is actually a function of my predominant

1

[behavior styles] personality types. For a time, I was confused about it. I thought my success could exist in a vacuum; that I could have my siloes of success over here, and when I was done establishing mine, I could help establish yours. It finally hit me that I was trying to establish a sort of cohabitation model of success where I would attempt to be successful alongside others whom I'd help. Now, for me it's a marriage. Your success is my success. When you achieve with my assistance, I achieve. This is the key to a durable model for success—helping others succeed."

Listen closely! This book is for the unsung heroes, the Chief Operating Officer (COO), Chief of Staff, Vice Presidents, General Managers, Senior Directors/Managers, Regional Managers/Directors, Associate Directors, Assistant/Deputy Directors, Program Managers, Team Leaders/Supervisors, and all those in support roles who ensure that the primary leader's vision becomes a reality. Your work behind the scenes transforms ideas into concrete action steps, propelling the organization forward.

In the daily grind, it's easy to overlook the vital importance of your role. But don't underestimate your impact: you are the backbone of leadership, providing essential guidance, coordination, and execution. This book will help you not only fulfill your responsibilities but thrive in your role, recognizing your power and influence.

Consider the human backbone, quietly supporting the body's movements. Like the backbone, you are often taken for granted, working diligently without recognition. This book aims to change that narrative, empowering you to embrace your role as the structure that holds everything together.

A brilliant CEO or other organizational leader can inspire with a vision, but it's you who turns that vision into reality. Your ability to provide stability, alignment, and drive is what moves the organization forward.

It's natural for the backbone to be overlooked when everything runs smoothly. People tend to focus on outcomes, not the underlying systems and people that make them possible. But remember, you are the driver behind the scenes, ensuring that the leader's vision is executed flawlessly.

Don't fall into the trap of thinking your role is less important because it's not in the spotlight. Your role is essential; without you, the vision remains a mere dream. It's time to change how you view your role and recognize the immense value you bring. You are not just carrying out tasks; you are the catalyst for success, empowering the entire organization.

Note: Pick up *The Backbone of Leadership Workbook: Embracing the Responsibility to Lead from Behind* **on Amazon or at www.TheBackboneofLeadership.com**

I HAVE A CONFESSION TO MAKE

I'm a self-proclaimed nerd—someone who is always searching for ways to increase my level of self-awareness and act from a space of healing. As I've worked through my own personal growth and leadership journey, I've come to realize that much of how I approach leadership and support stems from personal experiences, particularly those rooted in my childhood. But I also want to acknowledge that not everyone's approach to life or work is driven by adversity. There are many who are not necessarily impacted by Adverse Childhood Experiences (ACEs), and instead, their approach may be shaped by other drivers, including their behavior styles, values, or personal preferences.

For those of us who have experienced ACEs, the connection between those experiences and our roles today may be more direct. The CDC's ACE study found that 63.9% of U.S. adults reported at least one ACE, and 17.3% reported four or more. These early experiences can profoundly affect who we become in adulthood, particularly in how we relate to work, leadership, and relationships.

For me personally, I've discovered that witnessing family conflict, inconsistent parenting, abandonment, and social rejection are likely what drive my approach to leadership and the way I step into support roles. These experiences taught me to anticipate needs, create structure, and ensure stability—traits I've carried into my professional life. If any of this sounds familiar to you, there's a chance your past may be influencing your present in ways you haven't fully considered yet.

Many people who take on the role of the backbone of leadership—those who provide essential, behind-the-scenes support to ensure that everything runs smoothly—have a history that pushed them into these roles. It's not by accident. Early experiences often shape us into the reliable, steady individuals that teams and organizations come to depend on. If you've ever wondered why you're so good at supporting others and ensuring everything stays on track, it may be worth exploring how your past has influenced these skills.

Maybe you grew up in a home filled with conflict, where you had to be the peacemaker. Over time, you learned to calm situations and smooth things over before they escalated. That skill didn't just disappear—it followed you into adulthood, where you now find yourself in work environments keeping teams calm, managing tensions, and ensuring that the organization continues moving forward without chaos. Or perhaps you were raised in an environment where parenting was unpredictable—sometimes your needs were met, and other times, they weren't. This inconsistency likely pushed you to become hyper-aware of others' needs, always anticipating what might go wrong and working behind the scenes to prevent it.

It's important to note: this isn't about staying stuck in the past. It's about gaining clarity on how ACEs shaped us and recognizing that these skills—although developed out of necessity—are now valuable strengths. When you've experienced adversity as a child, you often learn to be the one who can manage stress, anticipate problems, and provide consistent support for others. That's the role of the backbone of leadership: you support, stabilize, and empower those around you.

Consider someone who, as a child, constantly witnessed family conflict. They may have taken on the role of peacemaker, managing the emotional climate to keep everyone else calm. Now, in their professional life, they find themselves doing the same thing—managing workplace tension, mediating conflicts, and ensuring that operations continue smoothly, even under stress. This wasn't just a skill they chose to develop; it was something they learned to survive, and now, it serves them and the organizations they support.

Or take the example of someone who experienced inconsistent or unpredictable parenting. As a child, they were never quite sure what to expect—whether their emotional needs would be met or ignored. As an adult, they might become the one who creates structure and stability in the workplace, ensuring that teams have what they need and that processes are followed to prevent the unpredictability they once experienced. Their need for control and stability stems from a childhood where things were anything but stable.

Then there's the person who experienced abandonment or loss as a child. Perhaps a parent left, or maybe there was an emotional absence in the home. Now, as an adult, this individual goes above and beyond to create environments of support and inclusion. They are the person in the office who makes sure everyone feels valued and appreciated, ensuring no one feels left behind. Their experiences have driven them to be the glue that holds the team together, always providing that extra layer of emotional or logistical support.

But I also recognize that not everyone's role

as the backbone of leadership is driven by adverse experiences. Many individuals bring a natural affinity for stability, support, and execution based on their behavior styles or personal preferences. Some people thrive in roles that require coordination and behind-the-scenes work simply because it aligns with their inherent strengths. These are people who may have always been inclined toward leadership support roles because they are organized, reliable, and enjoy ensuring that things run smoothly. Their drive doesn't come from trauma or past pain; it comes from a desire to see things done well and efficiently.

While these examples may sound familiar, I want to emphasize something critical: operating from a space of unhealed experiences will only lead to burnout. For years, I worked from that space—thinking I had to hold everything together because if I didn't, things would fall apart. But that kind of thinking is neither sustainable nor healthy. It's only when I began doing the hard work of healing that I realized I could still be the backbone of leadership, but in a healthier way. I could still provide support, but it didn't have to come at the cost of my own well-being.

That's why, throughout this book, I've intentionally used examples of healed individuals. I want you to see that even if you've been shaped by adversity, you can still operate from a place of healing. You can be the strong, steady support your team needs, without sacrificing your mental and emotional health. It's possible to be both supportive and whole, and that's the space I want to help you reach.

So, what drives you? Is it the desire to serve others, to be the steady force that keeps everything moving? Or is it the experiences of your past—maybe unresolved pain, insecurity, or fear—that push you to work harder, support more, and do it all without asking for recognition? I don't ask this to point fingers, but to encourage you to reflect on the source of your drive. Because here's the truth: if your work comes from a place of unresolved ACEs, it will eventually drain you. But if you do the work to heal and acknowledge the past, you can become even more powerful in your role.

Think about it: The CDC's study numbers I mentioned above are staggering, but they also remind us that we are not alone. Many of us are carrying the weight of our childhood experiences into our adult lives, and they are shaping how we show up at work, in relationships, and in leadership.

For example, someone who experienced social rejection or bullying as a child might now be the person in the office who goes out of their way to ensure everyone feels included and valued. They understand the pain of being left out and want to create a harmonious, inclusive environment where no one feels excluded. Their empathy, while rooted in past experiences of rejection, becomes a power for creating positive relationships in the workplace. But even empathy can become overwhelming if it's constantly being poured into others without proper boundaries.

On the other hand, if your behavior style naturally aligns with leadership support roles, your drive may come from a deep desire for structure, organization, and teamwork. People with a high Air Traffic Controller style often thrive on coordinating efforts, overseeing systems, and ensuring that everything operates with precision. They excel at logical analysis, detailed planning, and maintaining control over complex processes. Meanwhile, individuals with a high Grounds Crew style focus on creating a supportive, stable environment. They are attuned to the needs of the team, ensuring that daily operations run smoothly, and that everyone feels valued and equipped to succeed. These individuals don't necessarily carry the emotional weight of adverse experiences—they simply excel at keeping things in order and maintaining harmony because those are their natural strengths.

As for me, these two styles—Air Traffic Controller and Grounds Crew—are my dominant behavior styles. They shape how I approach leadership, structure, and team dynamics. Yet, I also have ACEs, as mentioned earlier, that have further influenced my approach to life and work. For more about behavior styles and the Flight Assessment, feel free to reach out to me at the email address provided in the final section of this book.

So, how do you know what drives you? It starts with self-awareness. Ask yourself, "What experiences shaped me into the person I am today?" And, please, tell yourself the truth! Maybe you recognize a piece of your story in the examples I've shared. Or perhaps there's something else in your past that has influenced how you lead and support others. Either way, the first step is recognizing it, and the second step is deciding how you want to move forward.

You have a choice. You can continue to be the backbone of leadership, providing stability and support to those around you. But I want you to do it from a place of strength and healing, not from a space of survival. You don't have to keep carrying the weight of your past alone.

In the pages that follow, I'll guide you through what it means to be the backbone of leadership—how to offer support, stabilize your teams, and empower others, all while maintaining your own sense of well-being. We'll explore how to manage crises, align teams with organizational goals, and cultivate future leaders. And we'll do it all with the understanding that your past, while significant, doesn't have to define your future.

My goal is to help you become the best version of yourself, both in leadership and in life. But that starts with being honest about what drives you. So, as you read this book, I want you to keep this question at the forefront of your mind: What drives you?

Let's commit to working from a space of healing, not survival. You have everything you need to be a powerful, impactful leader. Now let's take the next step—together.

I Have a Confession to Make

THE POWER OF STABILITY

In leadership, we often focus on the visionaries at the top—the ones who set grand strategies and inspire the workforce. But behind every successful leader is a foundation that quietly supports, enables, and stabilizes the organization. This foundation is you. Whether you're managing operations, aligning departments, or ensuring projects stay on course, your role is akin to the backbone of leadership. Just as the human backbone provides balance and structure, allowing the body to sit upright and steady, your leadership ensures that the organization moves forward with purpose and stickto-itiveness. Without your efforts, even the most brilliant vision can falter.

Think back to a time when you sat for hours at your desk, maybe late into the evening, going over the final details of a project. You might not have realized it, but your backbone was constantly at work, making tiny adjustments to keep you comfortable and balanced. It wasn't a passive act. Similarly, your role as a leader is far from passive. You're always observing, shifting, and tweaking to ensure everything runs smoothly. You're not just checking off to-do lists; you're providing the structural support that keeps the entire organization in balance.

Let me introduce you to Lisa M., a COO at a mid-sized marketing agency. Lisa had been with her company for over a decade, and her steady leadership had often been the anchor during turbulent times. Recently, the CEO launched an ambitious new growth plan to expand into international markets. While the vision was exciting, it created significant operational challenges. The sales department felt pressured to meet quotas in new territories, HR was overwhelmed with hiring, and finance was juggling the costs of managing international regulations and logistics.

Now, pause for a moment and ask yourself: If you were Lisa, how would you have approached this situation? Would you have focused on fixing one department first, or tried to overhaul the entire system? How would you have advised her to stabilize such a fast-moving, multi-layered challenge?

Lisa's first step was not to overhaul everything but to step back and assess the weak points. She should have taken time to evaluate where the foundation was still strong and where things were starting to crack under pressure. Much like how the backbone supports the body by making subtle, almost imperceptible adjustments, Lisa needed to stabilize the organization through a series of small, precise shifts. Coordinating cross-departmental meetings, reallocating resources to where they were needed most, and streamlining processes should have been the first steps. It wasn't flashy work, but it was essential to keeping everything aligned.

But Lisa's story goes beyond just her role in the organization—it's also about how her past shaped the way she approached these challenges. As a child, Lisa grew up in a household where emotional neglect was a constant. Her parents were busy and emotionally unavailable, often leaving her to manage her own needs. This shaped Lisa into someone who found value in being the person others could rely on, a role she carried with her into adulthood. She was always the one to keep things moving smoothly, to hold it all together—even at her own expense.

Here's a question for you: If you had worked with Lisa, would you have been able to see how her childhood experiences were impacting the way she led? Could you recognize her tendency to take on too much responsibility, driven by the need to be seen as dependable and in control?

What Lisa needed to do was recognize how these early experiences shaped her leadership style. Her tendency to take on too much—to be the one who kept everything running—was rooted in her childhood. As an adult, this led her to shoulder burdens she didn't need to carry. Lisa needed to learn how to delegate more effectively, to trust others, and to understand that she didn't have to prove her worth through constant self-sacrifice.

If you were in Lisa's shoes, how would you have managed the stress of balancing the needs of different departments while managing your own internal pressure to be everything for everyone?

Lisa began to learn that delegating wasn't a sign of weakness—it was a necessity for sustainable leadership. She recognized that while she had built her identity around being the person others could depend on, her true strength came from empowering her team to take on more responsibility. This allowed her to focus on what she did best—stabilizing the company's foundation and ensuring the vision stayed intact.

What would you have done if you were in

Lisa's position, facing the rapid growth of the company? Would you have focused on fixing the immediate problems, or taken a step back to think about the bigger picture?

Lisa should have focused on building stronger systems, rather than just addressing short-term problems. As the company expanded, the old processes that worked when they were a smaller operation no longer sufficed. Projects began slipping through the cracks, team members duplicated efforts, and frustrations mounted. Instead of allowing things to spiral, Lisa saw this as an opportunity to rebuild. She implemented project management tools, created clearer communication channels between teams, and delegated more responsibility to her department heads. In short, she didn't just fix the immediate problems—she rebuilt the company's framework to withstand future growth.

But Lisa's work didn't stop there. She also started to rebuild herself. Her past had left her with a sense of hyper-responsibility, a feeling that if she didn't handle everything herself, things would fall apart. But through self-reflection and personal development, Lisa learned to let go. She began to trust her team, recognizing that empowering others was not a threat to her own value, but evidence of her leadership.

If you were coaching Lisa, how would you help her recognize that trusting others could actually be a source of strength, not a loss of control?

Lisa's experience is a reminder that building strong systems isn't just about the organization—it's also about personal development. Leaders who focus on refining systems, improving processes, and empowering their teams are the ones who create environments where everyone can thrive. And sometimes, that starts with looking inward and recognizing what you need to let go of in order to move forward.

In Lisa's case, this meant recognizing that her desire to be the one everyone relied on came from her childhood experience of being emotionally overlooked. She had to learn that her worth wasn't tied to how much she did for others, but in how effectively she built a foundation that allowed the organization to grow—and how she built herself up in the process.

As you think about your own leadership journey, ask yourself: Where are you holding on too tightly? What responsibilities have you taken on because of your past, and how might letting go create space for you—and your organization—to grow?

As Lisa's company continued to expand, the inevitable crisis hit. The company's largest European partner went out of business, and the international expansion was thrown into jeopardy. Teams scrambled to recover, and the CEO's vision for growth hung in the balance.

In that moment of crisis, how would you have reacted? Would you have tried to fix everything at once, or focused on stabilizing the core operations?

Lisa remained calm. She prioritized key markets, reallocated resources, and ensured that communication between teams remained clear and productive. Her ability to maintain stability under pressure was crucial. She didn't panic. She trusted the systems she had built and the people she had empowered. This is where her leadership shined—not in grand gestures, but in the quiet, steady work of keeping the company moving forward.

Think back to a time when you faced a crisis in your organization. Did you try to solve everything at once, or did you focus on keeping the foundation strong? How would you have handled Lisa's situation differently, if at all?

In the end, Lisa's experience shows us that being the backbone of leadership isn't just about supporting others—it's about supporting yourself. It's about building a foundation that can bend without breaking, one that can adapt and grow, while staying true to the core values that guide your leadership.

So, as you reflect on your own leadership, ask yourself: Where can you step back and let others take more responsibility? What systems can you put in place to ensure long-term growth, not just short-term success? And how can you, like Lisa, find the balance between supporting your organization and taking care of yourself?

Shift Your Mind!

Mindset Shift 1: From Task-Oriented to Vision-Aligned

It's easy to get caught up in the day-to-day tasks that keep the organization running. But to truly make an impact, you need to shift your focus from simply checking off tasks to aligning everything you do with the leader's long-term vision. Your role is more than operational—it's strategic. Every system you build, every problem you solve, and every process you design should directly contribute to advancing the organization toward its ultimate goals.

What This Shift Means

This shift requires moving from a mindset focused on immediate tasks to one that prioritizes alignment with the bigger picture.

Instead of simply checking items off a to-do list, you become a key player in driving the organization forward by ensuring every action connects with the leader's vision. This transformation is about seeing yourself not as someone who maintains daily operations, but as a strategic architect whose actions have a long-term impact.

When you adopt a vision-aligned mindset, you are no longer just solving problems as they arise. Instead, you are preemptively designing processes and systems that will help the organization move toward its ultimate goals. You don't simply ask, "What needs to be done today?" You ask, "How does what we do today move us closer to our long-term objectives?" It's a shift from focusing on immediate tasks to ensuring that all efforts support the broader strategy.

By aligning your work with the vision, you enhance your strategic role within the organization. Every process you design and every system you oversee becomes an integral part of fulfilling the organization's goals. You take ownership of translating abstract ideas into real-world actions that drive growth and progress.

To-Dos

1. Schedule time with the CEO or primary leader to discuss their vision and long-term goals. Make sure you fully understand how your work ties into their big-picture strategy. Take notes on key objectives that will help you better align your systems with the overarching vision.

2. After your meeting, take a close look at the systems and processes you've put in place. Are they aligned with the leader's vision? Identify areas where adjustments can be made to better support long-term goals, then implement those changes.

3. Create a list of the top three organizational priorities that directly align with the leader's vision. Every week, review your work and ensure that these priorities are being addressed. If they're not, adjust your focus.

4. Once you're clear on the leader's vision, communicate it to your team. Help them see how their work contributes to the bigger picture. Regularly reference this vision in team meetings to keep everyone aligned.

Mindset Shift 2: From Invisible to Indispensable

As someone who ensures the organization's stability, your work can often go unnoticed—especially when everything is running smoothly. This can make you feel invisible or undervalued. However, the reality is that the less visible your work is, the more indispensable you are. You are the one who keeps the organization steady, allowing others to focus on their specific areas of expertise.

What This Shift Means

Shifting from feeling invisible to recognizing yourself as indispensable is about changing how you view your contributions to the organization. When everything is running smoothly, it's natural for people to overlook the systems and processes that enable that success, and as a result, your role might feel undervalued. But in reality, the less visible your work is, the more essential it has become—your behind-the-scenes contributions allow the organization to function seamlessly.

By adopting this mindset, you move from seeking recognition to embracing the importance of your steady, reliable presence. You are the stabilizing force that keeps everything moving forward, even when no one is actively noticing it. The ability to ensure that systems run without major disruptions means you are trusted implicitly to deliver. You are not invisible; you are the quiet strength that enables others to excel in their roles.

This shift in mindset empowers you to see yourself as a critical asset to the organization, even if you aren't in the spotlight. Your role as a stabilizer means that when things go well, it's because you've laid the groundwork. As you begin to recognize your indispensable nature, you'll naturally step into your authority and assert your value more confidently within the organization.

To-Dos

1. Keep a record of key milestones that you've achieved, focusing on how your systems and processes have contributed to the organization's stability and progress. Share these achievements with leadership during reviews or regular updates to remind them of the value you're bringing.

2. Set up regular check-ins with your team or peers to gather feedback on the effectiveness of the systems you've built. Use this feedback to make continuous improvements, but also as a way to measure and demonstrate your value to the organization.

3. When major projects or decisions are being made, don't hesitate to offer your input. Remind yourself that your voice is critical to maintaining the integrity and functional-

ity of the organization, and step up to provide insights when needed.

4. Start a daily or weekly practice of really considering your contributions. Even if they aren't publicly acknowledged, take pride in knowing that your work is essential to the organization's success. Keep a journal of your key accomplishments, and review it when you feel your work is being overlooked.

One of the most powerful shifts you can make is moving from a reactive mindset to a proactive one. Instead of waiting for problems to occur and then responding, anticipate challenges and prevent them from becoming roadblocks. This shift will not only enhance your effectiveness but will position you as a forward-thinking leader who can navigate the organization through uncertainties with ease.

What This Shift Means

Shifting from reactive to proactive leadership means you are no longer simply responding to issues after they arise, but instead are actively identifying potential risks and taking steps to prevent problems before they happen. This proactive mindset allows you to stay ahead of challenges rather than constantly playing catch-up.

Being reactive means waiting for things to go wrong and then scrambling to fix them—this can be draining and often leads to unnecessary disruptions. In contrast, a proactive mindset puts you in control. You become a strategist who not only solves problems but also predicts and avoids them altogether. This kind of leadership is forward-thinking, where you plan ahead, anticipate needs, and design systems that can adapt to changes.

When you shift to proactive thinking, you are constantly scanning the environment for risks, vulnerabilities, or opportunities to improve efficiency. You're no longer just waiting for things to break down—you're building resilience into every system you oversee. This approach makes you a more effective leader and provides the organization with greater stability, as you prevent fires from igniting in the first place. By thinking ahead, you position yourself as someone who drives success, rather than someone who merely manages crises.

To-Dos

1. Perform an audit of your current systems and processes to identify potential weak points. What risks could arise that may disrupt the stability of the organization? Make a list of the top 3-5 risks and create contingency plans for each.

2. Review your key systems and ensure they have built-in flexibility to adapt to change. Look for areas where you can streamline processes or introduce redundancies to prevent disruptions.

3. Schedule regular evaluations of your systems and processes (quarterly or biannually) to ensure they remain effective and aligned with the organization's goals. Proactively address any emerging issues before they escalate.

4. Make it a habit to stay informed

about external trends and internal developments that could impact the organization. Whether it's industry changes, new regulations, or shifts in leadership priorities, being ahead of the curve will allow you to adjust your approach before challenges arise.

Owning the Shift

Owning the shift from task-oriented to vision-aligned means embracing your role as a strategic leader, not just a task executor. Instead of focusing solely on completing daily operations, you begin to see every action, system, and process as a critical step in advancing the organization's long-term goals. This shift changes your perspective from reacting to immediate needs to actively contributing to the leader's broader vision, ensuring that everything you do aligns with and supports the future direction of the organization.

By fully adopting this mindset, you elevate your value within the organization. You are no longer just keeping things running—you're driving meaningful progress, ensuring that every task serves the larger mission. This proactive approach positions you as a key player in realizing the organization's goals, making you an indispensable part of the strategy.

2

THE POWER OF STANDING TALL

Let's take a step back and think about how the backbone keeps us upright, stable, and balanced. Now, imagine the backbone being out of alignment, even just a little. The body feels off, and movements become difficult or painful. Similarly, in an organization, alignment with the leader's vision is critical. It keeps the organization moving forward, focused on its goals, and adaptable to challenges. Without this alignment, things start to fall apart: teams lose focus, efforts become fragmented, and the organization struggles to move in a unified direction.

Your role is to be that backbone, keeping

everything connected to the bigger picture. You don't just ensure tasks are getting done. Your responsibility is deeper—you need to make sure that every action, every team, and every process connects to the overarching vision. When all parts of an organization move together in alignment, it's like a well-coordinated body. But when parts are out of sync, you end up with a disjointed, uncoordinated mess, no different than trying to walk with one leg moving forward while the other stays behind. Sooner or later, you're going to fall.

Alignment brings clarity and strength. It ensures that everyone knows not just what to do but why they're doing it. It connects their daily efforts to the larger goals of the organization. Without it, even the most well-meaning teams can veer off course, leading to conflict, wasted resources, and missed opportunities.

Consider the experience of Michael R., the COO of a retail company undergoing rapid growth. The company was expanding fast, but things weren't moving smoothly.

Departments began to drift from the core vision: engineering focused on developing new features, marketing prioritized customer acquisition, and customer service was overwhelmed with complaints they couldn't keep up with. The lack of alignment began to show, creating friction and slowing down progress. Everyone was busy, but no one was working in unison toward the company's goals.

Now, put yourself in Michael's shoes. How would you have approached this growing disconnection between departments? Would you have focused on one problem at a time, or would you have looked at the larger picture and tried to bring everyone back into alignment?

Michael was no stranger to handling instability. Growing up, his household was marked by uncertainty. His father struggled with alcohol, leading to erratic behavior—sometimes he was present and loving, and at other times, he disappeared for days. As a child, Michael learned early on how to create structure where there was none. This gave him a unique ability to quickly recognize when things were out of alignment and the need to fix problems before they escalated.

In his current role, Michael applied these skills to bring the organization back into alignment. Rather than overhauling entire systems, he realized that small, well-placed adjustments could make a significant impact. He spent extra time with the CEO, not just listening to the broad vision but asking more specific questions that clarified the leader's expectations. This deeper understanding allowed him to translate the CEO's vision into something concrete for the departments to follow.

If you were Michael, how would you have communicated this newfound clarity to your teams? Would you have held individual meetings with department heads, or brought everyone together to reestablish alignment?

Michael chose to initiate vision-alignment sessions with the department leaders. Instead of micromanaging, he brought the heads of engineering, marketing, and customer service together to connect their goals back to the company's overarching vision. He understood that alignment couldn't happen in silos—it had to be a collective effort. He facilitated conversations that highlighted how each department's work contributed to the larger picture.

What should Michael have done next to ensure that these conversations turned into long-lasting change within the company?

Michael should have set up regular cross-departmental meetings to ensure ongoing alignment. He created spaces for open dialogue, allowing departments to share their progress and how their work aligned with the company's strategic goals. In these meetings, he didn't simply enforce directives—he listened to the challenges each department faced and worked collaboratively to find solutions. By fostering this continuous communication, he made sure that alignment wasn't a one-time event but an ongoing process.

One of the key things Michael had to

address was how the company's rapid growth was causing miscommunication between teams. Engineering wanted more time to perfect new features, while marketing pushed for faster rollouts, and customer service was overwhelmed with the volume of calls. Michael understood that for the company to move forward, these departments needed to work in harmony, not independently.

How would you have handled the friction between these departments? Would you have intervened early on or allowed them to try to resolve the issues themselves?

Michael stepped in early to realign the teams, recognizing that allowing misalignment to persist would only create further delays and frustration. He encouraged them to understand each other's objectives and the broader company goals. This communication helped teams see how their efforts were interdependent and led to more collaboration across departments.

Michael's approach to alignment didn't just stop with communication. Once the teams understood the vision, he needed to make it actionable. I often tell leaders that vision without execution is just a dream. Michael's next step was to break the CEO's vision down into manageable, achievable steps for each department. He created clear, strategic roadmaps with short-term goals that allowed the teams to focus on immediate actions while still contributing to the long-term vision.

For example, the CEO's vision was to become a customer-first brand within two years. Michael set incremental goals to achieve this: first, improving the customer feedback system; second, integrating customer feedback into product development; and third, updating the marketing strategy to reflect a more customer-centric approach.

If you were Michael, how would you have set these goals for your team? Would you have taken a similar approach by breaking them down into smaller, more achievable milestones?

By breaking the broader vision into concrete

steps, Michael ensured that no one felt over-whelmed by the scope of the project. Instead, each team understood how their daily tasks contributed to the company's long-term success. This approach gave them the clarity they needed to move forward with purpose and stay motivated.

Another key challenge Michael faced was ensuring that alignment wasn't just achieved but maintained. Alignment isn't something you fix once and forget about. It requires ongoing attention and fine-tuning. As teams evolve and new challenges arise, the alignment can start to drift.

How would you have ensured that alignment remained intact over time? Would you have set up regular check-ins, or waited for signs of misalignment before intervening?

Michael wisely chose to keep his finger on the pulse, scheduling regular check-ins with department heads to ensure that alignment was maintained. He understood that waiting for problems to arise would only lead to bigger issues down the road. By staying proactive, he was able to make small adjustments to keep the organization on course.

One thing that helped Michael was his ability to anticipate potential misalignments before they became serious problems. His upbringing had taught him to be sensitive to signs of instability, and he applied that awareness to his work. He could sense when teams were beginning to drift and took quick action to realign them. This foresight allowed the company to stay flexible, even during times of rapid growth.

Finally, ask yourself: What would you have done if, despite your best efforts, misalignment still occurred? Would you have started over from scratch, or made small adjustments to bring things back into balance?

Michael didn't overreact when misalignment happened. Instead, he treated it like a small slip in posture—something that could be corrected with minor adjustments rather than drastic changes. He didn't need to rebuild the entire organization from the ground up. He just needed to remind the teams of their shared goals and how their work aligned with the leader's vision. By addressing misalignment early and making targeted corrections, Michael kept the company moving forward.

Michael's experience shows that being the backbone of leadership means more than just overseeing tasks. It's about ensuring alignment—keeping the organization connected to its vision and moving in the same direction. His story is a reminder that alignment isn't a one-time achievement but an ongoing process of adjustment, communication, and collaboration. It's about understanding the leader's vision at a deep level, translating it into practical steps, and continuously checking in to make sure everything stays on track.

As you reflect on Michael's experience, think about your own leadership role. Where might misalignment be creeping into your organization? How can you ensure that your teams are not just working hard, but working in unison toward the same goal? And most importantly, what small adjustments can you make today to bring everything back into alignment and keep your organization standing tall, focused, and adaptable?

Shift Your Mind!

Mindset Shift 1: From Executor to Interpreter of Vision

It's easy to fall into the trap of thinking that your role is just about executing tasks and making sure operations run smoothly. However, your true value lies in being an interpreter of the leader's vision. The CEO or leader often communicates in broad, ambitious terms. It's your job to not only understand the vision but to translate it into clear, actionable strategies that teams can follow.

What This Shift Means

Instead of simply focusing on "getting things done," you must shift your focus to interpreting and clarifying the vision for every level of the organization. Think of yourself as a bridge between the visionary and the teams on the ground, helping everyone understand how their specific roles and actions contribute to the greater goal.

To-Dos

1. Set up consistent, meaningful conversations with the CEO or primary leader to clarify any ambiguity in the vision. Make sure you fully grasp their goals, priorities, and values.

2. Take the high-level vision and break it down into language and objectives that resonate with different teams. Tailor your communication to each department so that everyone understands their part in achieving the vision.

3. Don't just assume everyone gets the vision—actively seek feedback to ensure teams are aligned and fully understand the bigger picture.

Mindset Shift 2: From Maintaining Order to Creating Purpose

Often, those in support roles view their job as maintaining order, ensuring systems run smoothly, and addressing immediate operational needs. But to foster real alignment, you need to go beyond merely keeping things running—you need to help people find purpose in their work by connecting their day-to-day activities to the organization's broader mission.

What This Shift Means

Move from being a taskmaster to being a purpose-driver. Your role isn't just to maintain processes; it's to make sure that every employee understands why their work matters in the grand scheme of things. By consistently connecting tasks and goals to the vision, you'll help build stronger alignment and boost morale.

To-Dos

1. In meetings and updates, make it a point to consistently tie team efforts back to the broader organizational mission. Show how each department's work directly impacts the success of the overall vision.
2. Recognize and celebrate the moments when teams contribute to significant progress toward the vision. Help them see that their

work is more than just tasks—it's part of a larger journey.

3. Encourage team members to share how they think their work aligns with the company's mission. This helps them internalize their purpose and feel connected to the bigger picture.

Mindset Shift 3: From Reactive to Proactive Alignment Keeper

It's common for leaders in support roles to spend much of their time reacting to misalignment when it occurs—whether it's departments working at cross-purposes, teams drifting from their goals, or resources being wasted on non-strategic efforts. However, to truly ensure alignment, you must shift from reacting to these issues as they arise to proactively keeping alignment strong from the outset.

What This Shift Means

Rather than waiting for misalignment to happen and then fixing it, make alignment an ongoing priority. This requires constant communication, regular check-ins, and fostering a culture that prioritizes collaboration and shared goals. By maintaining alignment continuously, you prevent the kind of organizational drift that wastes resources and dilutes the leader's vision.

To-Dos

1. Schedule periodic check-ins with department heads and teams to ensure everyone remains aligned with the company's mission. Address any potential shifts in focus before they become larger issues.

2. Be on the lookout for early signs of misalignment—whether it's a project that seems out of sync with broader goals or teams that aren't communicating well. Nip these issues in the bud before they become disruptive.

3. Create opportunities for teams to work together and share insights. When different parts of the organization collaborate, it's easier to keep everyone focused on the larger mission and avoid silos that can lead to

misalignment.

Owning the Shift

These mindset shifts—becoming an inter-preter of vision, a creator of purpose, and a proactive alignment keeper—will elevate your role and help you ensure that the orga-nization stands tall in alignment with its vision. By shifting how you approach your responsibilities, you'll not only keep teams focused but also foster a sense of purpose and unity that will propel the organization toward its goals.

Embrace these shifts, and you'll find yourself leading from a position of strength, ensur-ing that every part of the organization moves cohesively toward the future that the leader has envisioned.

3

THE POWER OF TURNING VISION INTO ACTION

Think about walking forward—each movement purposeful and coordinated. Beneath that smooth motion is the backbone, holding everything together, maintaining balance, and providing the structure necessary for movement. Without the backbone's support, walking would be impossible. Similarly, in an organization, you—whether you're in a role as Vice President, COO, or any other key support position—are the backbone that drives execution. You ensure that the organization moves from strategy to action, step by step, toward its goals. I know I keep saying this, but you need to get it.

Without your efforts to manage operations, resources, and teams, the organization would struggle to turn vision into reality. It would remain stagnant, stuck in planning, unable to make progress. In this chapter, we'll explore how you, as the backbone of execution, make sure that plans become action and the organization moves forward toward its goals. We'll also look closely at the challenges you may face, especially if your behavior style is more relational than operational, like those with a high Flight Attendant style. By focusing on how these strengths can be harnessed, even in execution-focused roles, we'll see how self-awareness can turn potential obstacles into assets.

Execution is where everything comes to life. A strategy or a compelling vision without execution is nothing more than wishful thinking. It's one thing to have an ambitious goal or a well-crafted plan, but without follow-through, those plans stay confined to the whiteboard. Execution is where ideas take form—where they move from concept to reality.

Let's take the story of Leah S., a Vice President of Operations at a growing tech company. Leah has a high Flight Attendant behavior style, which means she thrives on relationships, communication (not necessarily timely, or perfectly clear, but you get the point), and creating an environment of collaboration. People gravitate toward her because of her ability to connect emotionally, build trust, and inspire teams to work together. However, when it comes to execution, Leah sometimes struggles. With her natural inclination to focus on relationships, she finds herself caught up in resolving interpersonal issues, ensuring everyone feels heard, and creating harmony between departments.

If you were in Leah's position, how would you handle the balance between fostering strong relationships and driving execution? Would you focus on the operational side or try to find a way to balance both?

Leah's focus on relationships is invaluable in fostering a collaborative culture, but in execution, she faced challenges because her attention often shifted toward making people feel comfortable rather than pushing for deadlines and operational efficiency. Instead of abandoning her relational strengths, Leah should have developed a system where she could integrate her focus on people with the necessary discipline to meet goals. Leaders like Leah can harness their relational strengths by framing execution as something that benefits both people and the organization. Execution is not the enemy of relationships—it can, in fact, strengthen them by creating clear expectations and shared success.

One of the most challenging aspects of driving execution is translating the leader's broad vision into specific, actionable steps. Leaders often think in long-term, high-level concepts. But for that vision to become reality, it needs to be broken down into day-to-day operations that move the organization forward incrementally. This is where Leah's leadership shines—when she's able to bridge the gap between vision and action through collaboration.

In Leah's company, the CEO envisioned the organization becoming a leader in tech-driven products over the next five years. Leah loved the concept and was excited about rallying the teams around it. Her Flight Attendant style kicked in immediately—she called meetings, got everyone pumped, and fostered a lot of enthusiasm about what could be achieved. But when it came to executing on the details, things started to stall.

Would you have focused on keeping morale high or shifted your attention to ensuring that clear, actionable steps were in place to meet deadlines?

Leah's challenge was focus. Being people-oriented, she often struggled with the operational side of turning ideas into processes. She thrived on brainstorming and relationship-building but had trouble translating those lofty ideas into concrete actions with deadlines, responsibilities, and metrics. This is where the execution gap appeared.

Leah didn't need to abandon her strengths—just adapt them. She could have developed a structured plan that maintained her team's enthusiasm but also added clear timelines and accountability. Leah needed to set up regular cross-department check-ins where her relational strengths created a motivating and engaging environment while keeping everyone focused on deadlines. By breaking down large goals into smaller, actionable steps, Leah could have ensured progress while maintaining team morale.

One of Leah's biggest strengths was her ability to coordinate people and create connections between teams. However, her natural tendency to avoid conflict and ensure everyone is happy often led to delays when tough decisions were required. Execution requires alignment and clear direction, and sometimes that means making hard choices or cutting through disagreements quickly to keep things on track.

Take, for example, a major product launch Leah was overseeing. The engineering team wanted more time to perfect the product, while marketing was pushing for a quicker launch to capture market demand. Leah found herself in the middle, trying to keep both sides happy. Her instinct was to smooth things over, to listen to everyone's concerns, and avoid creating tension. But with the launch date looming, there was no time for prolonged discussions.

How would you have handled this situation? Would you have prioritized one team over the other, or found a way to keep everyone aligned without delaying the launch?

Leah should have made the tough call to prioritize marketing's timeline while ensuring engineering had clear milestones to address post-launch issues quickly. She needed to communicate the decision with both empathy and firmness, keeping her teams engaged and on track. Leaders in similar situations must recognize that execution isn't just about meeting deadlines—it's about making tough, informed decisions that keep the organization moving forward. Balancing relationships with operational rigor is key.

Operations is where Leah really started to grow. Initially, she felt overwhelmed by the complexities of managing resources, time-lines, and expectations. Her instinct was to delegate operational details so she could focus on her relational strengths. But as the company expanded, Leah recognized that her direct involvement in operations was essential for ensuring success.

Leah should have seen operations as the engine that kept her teams aligned with the vision. Instead of viewing them as purely technical or detail-heavy, she needed to reframe operations as an extension of her leadership, where she could create systems that not only met the company's goals but also empowered her people.

What would you have done differently to manage the operational complexities? Would you have taken a hands-on approach, or continued to delegate operational tasks?

Leah could have become more proactive in setting up operational frameworks that allowed her teams to function smoothly. She needed to implement project management tools that provided transparency without micromanaging. Operations should have been viewed as a system that combined structure with motivation, where progress was measured, and teams felt supported at every stage.

Another important shift Leah needed to make was blending her emotional intelligence with data-driven decision-making. Execution isn't just about relationships or numbers—it's about integrating both. Leah should have used her relational strengths to build strong connections with her teams but also started relying more on data to track progress and adjust strategies. This balance would have given her a more complete view of how her organization was performing and allowed her to make informed decisions.

Leah's ability to inspire her teams was one of her greatest assets. But inspiration alone doesn't get the job done. Leaders need to provide structure, clear expectations, and accountability systems. Regular check-ins and progress reports would have kept her teams aligned with the company's vision while tracking their contributions toward the end goal.

Execution isn't just about completing tasks—it's about ensuring that every action is aligned with the company's vision. What steps would you take to create accountability systems without stifling creativity and enthusiasm?

Leah could have blended her people-first approach with the discipline of execution. It's not about becoming rigid or cold—it's about finding the right balance between motivating your team and holding them accountable for results. Leah didn't have to give up who she was—she just needed to be more strategic in applying her strengths to drive execution.

Execution also requires resilience, and Leah faced several challenges along the way. One of her biggest hurdles was her tendency to avoid conflict, which often delayed important decisions. Leaders in similar situations must learn that avoiding tough conversations only holds back progress. Transparent, productive conversations lead to quicker, more effective decisions.

Another challenge Leah faced was maintaining momentum over long-term projects. Flight Attendants, like Leah, are great at generating enthusiasm at the start, but they can sometimes struggle to keep that energy going. Leaders need systems that keep teams engaged throughout the entire project lifecycle, setting smaller goals and celebrating milestones to maintain morale.

How would you keep your team's energy and focus over long-term projects? Would you celebrate all wins along the way, or push for continuous progress?

Leah's growth story highlights an important lesson: your natural behavior style doesn't limit your ability to execute—it simply shapes how you approach it. Execution isn't about forgetting about who you are; it is, however, about leveraging your strengths in new ways to ensure results. Leah transformed her company's ability to execute on its goals by blending her relational focus with operational rigor.

As the backbone of leadership, you play a critical role in driving execution, coordinating efforts across teams, managing operations, and leading your teams to success. By taking a proactive, strategic approach to execution, you ensure that the organization doesn't just move, but moves in the right direction, one purposeful step at a time.

What would you do to ensure your organization is moving in the right direction? Would you focus on strategic planning, operational efficiency, or balancing both?

The key to driving execution lies in balance—balancing relationships with results, inspiration with accountability, and vision with action. When done right, you help transform vision into reality, creating lasting success for the organization and everyone within it.

Shift Your Mind!

Mindset Shift 1: From Executor to Orchestrator

It's easy to think of your role as someone

who simply ensures that tasks get done. However, to truly drive execution, you must shift from being a task-focused executor to an orchestrator of coordinated efforts across teams. Your job is not just about ensuring that work gets completed but about making sure that every action aligns with the organization's overall strategy and contributes to the leader's vision. Think harmony in music—you know, orchestration.

What This Shift Means

Instead of viewing execution as a series of independent tasks, see yourself as an orchestrator, coordinating multiple moving parts to achieve a unified result. This requires understanding the interconnections between teams, resources, and timelines, and making sure that every effort is in harmony with the overall objectives. You become the conductor of a symphony, ensuring that each section of the organization plays its part at the right time and in the right way to achieve the desired outcome.

To-Dos
1. Regularly check in with different

departments to ensure their work aligns with the overall strategy. Create opportunities for cross-functional collaboration and make sure everyone is moving toward the same goal.

2. Identify where teams rely on each other and ensure that those dependencies are managed effectively. Anticipate potential roadblocks that may arise if one team falls behind, and address them proactively.

3. Break down long-term goals into smaller, coordinated milestones. This helps keep teams aligned and focused on moving forward step by step.

Mindset Shift 2: From Operations Manager to Strategic Driver

As a leader overseeing execution, it's natural to focus on managing day-to-day operations. However, to truly move the organization forward, you need to elevate your thinking from operations management to strategic driving. Your role is not just about keeping things running smoothly—it's about actively pushing the organization toward its long-term goals, ensuring that every decision you make contributes to the broader strategy.

What This Shift Means

Instead of seeing operations as something to be maintained, see them as a vehicle for achieving the leader's vision. You are no longer just a manager of existing systems—you are a strategic leader, using operations to drive the organization toward its goals. This shift allows you to move from simply managing processes to actively shaping them in a way that supports growth and success.

To-Dos

1. Constantly ask yourself how each operational process supports the leader's broader vision. If a process isn't contributing to the strategic goals, consider revising, streamlining, or completely getting rid of it.
2. Use data and metrics to inform your decisions about resource allocation,

project prioritization, and team performance. Data will help you see
where adjustments are needed to
stay on track with the strategy.
3. When managing daily operations,
keep the long-term goals in mind.
Make decisions that not only solve
immediate challenges but also set
the stage for future success.

Mindset Shift 3: From Problem Solver to Anticipator of Roadblocks

It's common for leaders driving execution to
focus on solving problems as they arise.
However, a proactive mindset shift from
problem solver to anticipator of roadblocks
can elevate your effectiveness significantly.
Instead of waiting for challenges to occur
and then reacting to them, you must anticipate potential issues before they become
full-blown obstacles. This shift allows you to
prevent delays, minimize disruptions, and
keep execution moving forward seamlessly.

What This Shift Means

Moving from a reactive approach to a proactive one means you're constantly scanning the horizon for risks, bottlenecks, or inefficiencies that could hinder the organization's progress. Rather than firefighting, you become a strategic leader who plans ahead, identifies potential roadblocks early, and puts contingencies in place to keep things running smoothly. You become not just a problem solver, but a strategist who ensures that problems are minimized or avoided entirely.

To-Dos

1. Frequently assess ongoing projects and operational processes for potential risks or areas where bottlenecks could develop. By identifying weak points early, you can address them before they become major issues.

2. For critical projects and processes, develop backup plans so that if roadblocks arise, the organization can pivot without losing momentum.

3. Encourage your teams to think ahead and identify potential chal-

lenges in their areas of responsibility. Create an environment where proactive problem-solving is valued and rewarded.

4. Stay informed about external factors—such as market trends, economic changes, or shifts in customer preferences—that could impact execution. Adjust your plans as necessary to avoid being blindsided by unexpected challenges.

Owning the Shift

These three mindset shifts—from executor to orchestrator, from operations manager to strategic driver, and from problem solver to anticipator of roadblocks—are essential for effectively driving execution and ensuring that the organization moves forward with purpose. By adopting these shifts, you'll not only ensure that tasks are completed, but you'll also create a more coordinated, strategic, and proactive approach to execution that will help the organization achieve its long-term vision.

When you shift your perspective from focusing on the immediate to thinking more holistically and strategically, you'll find yourself not just managing the day-to-day but truly driving the organization's progress. Embrace these shifts, and you'll play a crucial role in ensuring that the leader's vision becomes a reality, moving the organization forward one step at a time with intention and precision.

The Power of Turning Vision into Action

4

THE POWER OF FLEXIBILITY

I am going to do my best to illustrate the power of flexibility with Megan B.'s story, which takes place during a time when the entire healthcare industry was grappling with a rapidly changing landscape. Like many in her position, Megan, a mid-level manager at a regional healthcare provider, found herself in uncharted waters. The pandemic had wreaked havoc on her organization, a smaller healthcare provider in a community where larger hospitals were starting to dominate. Yet, while those larger institutions had the resources to pivot more quickly, Megan's organization had something else: deep, personal connections with the community. That was their strength, and Megan knew it was something they had to protect, even while adapting to a rapidly evolving environment.

Megan's background played a huge role in how she approached these challenges. Growing up as an only child in a home where one of her parents struggled with alcoholism, she learned early on how to navigate difficult and unpredictable situations. In many ways, she had been preparing for moments like this all her life. The uncertainty at home taught her the importance of flexibility—how to adapt to changes she couldn't control—but it also taught her the need for stability and strength. These skills became her backbone as a leader.

At the time, her healthcare organization was under immense pressure. The pandemic had accelerated changes in the industry, and larger hospitals in the area were expanding their services, attracting patients, and investing in advanced technologies. Megan's provider couldn't compete with them on resources, and the leadership team was unsure of how to move forward. Some leaders were pushing to cut costs and services to stay afloat, while others wanted to invest in new technologies to keep up with the competition. There was a growing sense of panic.

If you were in Megan's shoes, how would you have approached these competing priorities? Would you have chosen to cut costs or invest in technology? Or would you have looked for a middle path?

Megan, drawing from her own experiences, knew that bending too far to either extreme would lead to breaking. In her childhood, she had seen how important it was to maintain stability in the face of chaos. That stability wasn't about being rigid, though—it was about being flexible enough to adapt while staying grounded in what really mattered.

The organization's strength lay in its personalized care, its connection to the community. Megan realized that this was the foundation they needed to protect, no matter how much they adapted to the changes around them. Larger hospitals couldn't offer that same intimate, local connection. They had scale, but her provider had trust and a deep relationship with patients. Megan believed that leaning into that strength would give them an edge, even as they faced challenges.

Do you think focusing on personalized care is enough in the face of larger competition, or would you have considered a different approach?

Megan's ability to see this comes from her own life experience. Growing up with the unpredictability of her parent's addiction meant that she constantly had to make adjustments, but she never lost sight of the fact that certain things, like emotional stability, were non-negotiable. That's exactly what she did for her organization—she was flexible where she needed to be but held firm where it mattered most.

At the same time, Megan understood that clinging too tightly to old ways of doing things could lead to stagnation. The health-care industry was evolving rapidly, and the organization needed to adapt. So, she sought a middle path. Instead of abandoning their core values of personalized care, Megan worked with her team to find ways they could modernize without losing the personal touch that made them stand out.

Megan started small. She didn't rush to implement sweeping changes but instead focused on a few key areas where flexibility could be introduced gradually. One of the first things she did was implement a telehealth option for patients. Many larger hospitals had been offering telehealth for years, but Megan's team had resisted, fearing it would undermine the personal relationships they had built with patients. However, during the pandemic, telehealth became essential for continuing care, especially for their most vulnerable patients who were hesitant to visit the clinic in person.

Megan was strategic in how she rolled this out. Rather than just introducing telehealth as a new service, she framed it as an extension of the personal care they already provided. She trained her team to continue offering the same level of personalized service during virtual visits as they would during in-person appointments. They took extra time to connect with patients, ensuring that the technology didn't get in the way of the human touch. The result? Patients felt cared for, even in a virtual setting, and the organization found a new way to serve their community while adapting to a post-pandemic world.

Would you have implemented telehealth earlier in the pandemic, or waited like Megan to ensure that the personalized care aspect wasn't lost?

Her decision to embrace telehealth wasn't just about jumping on a trend—it was about recognizing that flexibility didn't have to mean giving up what made them special. Instead, they could bend in a way that allowed them to better serve their patients while maintaining the core of their identity. This is one of the most important lessons for anyone in a leadership support role. You are the ones who must guide your organization in adapting to new realities without losing sight of its core mission.

Megan's approach also extended to internal operations. As the pandemic receded and restrictions loosened, there was a push from some parts of the organization to return to the pre-pandemic way of doing things. But Megan knew better. The world had changed, and they couldn't just go back to how things were. Instead, she encouraged her team to keep some of the pandemic-era innovations that had worked well. For example, they had streamlined their administrative processes during the pandemic to reduce physical contact, and those changes made things more efficient for both staff and patients. So, Megan made those changes permanent.

Yet, she didn't force these changes from the top down. Growing up in a chaotic household had taught Megan the importance of buy-in—people are more likely to support change when they feel involved in the process. She invited her team to offer feedback, asking them what had worked during the pandemic and what hadn't. By making her team a part of the decision-making process, Megan ensured that the changes felt like a collective effort, not just another top-down directive.

Do you agree that engaging the team in decision-making is key to implementing lasting changes, or would you have taken a more directive-style approach?

Megan's ability to lead through this transition highlights a key lesson for anyone in leadership support roles: flexibility is not about abandoning tradition, nor is it about blindly following trends. It's about understanding when change is necessary and finding ways to bend that still honor the organization's core values. Leaders like Megan need to be both the backbone that keeps the organization upright and the flexibility that allows it to twist without breaking.

But Megan's story also reminds us that flexibility must be paired with strength. As the pandemic wound down and patients began returning to in-person appointments, Megan's organization faced renewed pressure from larger hospitals that had recovered faster from the crisis. Some in her leadership team began suggesting further cuts to services, but Megan held firm. She knew that if they cut too deeply, they would lose what made them special—their ability to offer personalized, high-quality care.

In those moments, Megan relied on the same inner strength that had carried her through the uncertainty of her childhood. Just as she had learned to provide stability for herself in the face of chaos, she provided that same stability for her team, even as external pressures mounted. She was flexible in her approach to adapting to the changing landscape, but she never lost sight of the organization's foundation. And that is the true essence of leadership support—knowing when to bend and when to stand firm.

If you were facing similar external pressures, how would you balance the need for cost-cutting with the need to protect core values?

As someone in a support role, this balance between flexibility and strength is critical. You're the one who ensures that the organization can adapt without losing its identity. Megan's story shows that you don't have to choose between innovation and tradition—you can have both, as long as you are strategic about how you implement change.

Megan didn't fully solve the problem of how to compete with larger hospitals. That challenge remains, but she has laid the foundation for her organization to thrive in the face of adversity. By holding fast to the core values that make them unique while remaining flexible enough to adapt to new challenges, Megan's team is navigating a post-pandemic world with courage.

What would you have done differently if you were in Megan's role? How would you have approached the challenge of competing with larger, better-resourced hospitals?

Megan's story reminds us that being in a leadership support role requires both flexibility and strength. You are the backbone of the organization, the one who ensures that it stands firm while adapting to new realities. And while the road ahead may be uncertain, if you can balance the need for flexibility with the need to protect your organization's core values, you can help it bend without breaking.

For those of you reading this, remember Megan's story the next time your organization faces a major challenge. You don't have to sacrifice your foundation to adapt—find the balance, and you'll help your organization thrive even in the most difficult of circumstances.

Shift Your Mind!

Mindset Shift 1: From Fixed Plans to Dynamic Strategies

It's easy to become attached to a fixed plan, but in a world of constant change, you must shift from rigid planning to dynamic strategy-building. While having a plan is essential, recognize that sticking to it without flexibility can lead to stagnation. Instead, develop strategies that are adaptable as new information, challenges, or opportunities arise.

What This Shift Means

Rather than viewing plans as static, see

them as living frameworks that can evolve when necessary. This shift allows you to be open to change while still keeping your core objectives intact. Instead of simply following a set path, you'll lead with strategic agility, ready to adjust course without sacrificing long-term goals.

To-Dos

1. Schedule regular reviews of organizational plans and strategies to assess if they still align with the current environment and goals. Look for areas where flexibility is needed and be open to making necessary adjustments.

2. Foster a culture where teams are encouraged to adapt their approaches when they encounter new challenges. Allow them to provide input on how strategies can evolve to stay relevant.

3. Develop contingency plans that allow you to pivot quickly when external factors shift. This can include scenario planning, where you anticipate potential challenges

and determine alternative approaches.

Mindset Shift 2: From Reactive Adjustments to Proactive Adaptation

While reactive adjustments are often necessary during crises, you should aim to shift from making changes reactively to proactively anticipating the need for adaptation. This involves continuously monitoring internal and external developments to prepare for changes before they impact the organization.

What This Shift Means

Instead of reacting to disruption only after it occurs, adopt a forward-looking approach. This shift enables you to proactively identify trends, risks, or opportunities, so you can prepare to pivot in advance. By doing this, you make flexibility a strength rather than a last-minute scramble to adjust.

To-Dos
1. Regularly review market trends, technological advancements, and

competitive shifts. This will help you anticipate changes that might affect the organization, giving you time to prepare.

2. Evaluate areas of the organization that might be vulnerable to changes or disruptions. Identify potential risks and plan preventive measures to stay ahead of them.

3. Set up a system of early indicators (both internal and external) that signal when adjustments might be necessary. This could be performance metrics, customer feedback, or external economic indicators.

Mindset Shift 3: From Rigidity to Resilient Flexibility

Shifting from a rigid approach to resilient flexibility means understanding that strength doesn't mean rigidity. Resilience comes from maintaining a strong foundation (core principles) while being able to adapt strategies, processes, and resources when necessary.

What This Shift Means

This shift allows you to maintain the strength to uphold the organization's vision and values while empowering you to adapt when needed. Resilient flexibility is about knowing which parts of the organization must remain constant and which parts can change. By understanding this balance, you ensure that the organization can thrive amid change without losing its foundation.

To-Dos

1. Clearly define which aspects of the organization must remain constant, such as core values, vision, and long-term goals. Ensure that these guide decision-making and remain steady even as other areas flex.

2. Create systems and processes that are resilient but adaptable. These systems should have the ability to scale, pivot, or adjust as the organization grows or external conditions change.

3. Promote a culture of continuous learning where team members are encouraged to explore new ideas, experiment with solutions, and

share insights. This helps foster resilience by allowing the organization to adapt and innovate in the face of challenges.

Owning the Shift

By adopting these three mindset shifts—dynamic strategy-building, proactive adaptation, and resilient flexibility—you will not only help your organization navigate changes but also position it for long-term success. The to-dos outlined here provide practical steps to ensure that your role balances both the flexibility to pivot and the strength to stay grounded in core objectives. By owning this balance, you can lead your teams and the organization through uncertainty with confidence and resilience.

5

THE POWER OF WELL-COORDINATED COMMUNICATION

Imagine twisting your body without the coordination of your backbone—it would be disjointed and inefficient, possibly even painful. The backbone allows for proper movement and coordination between different parts of the body, keeping everything aligned and functioning harmoniously. In an organization, communication and coordination play a similar role. They are the invisible structures that keep the operation working smoothly, aligning every team's efforts with the larger goals of the organization. Without communication and coordination, even the best strategies will falter.

Now, think of an individual in a leadership support role, specifically someone like Jason K., a Communication Director at a large non-profit organization during the pandemic. Jason had a high Air Traffic Controller and Grounds Crew behavior style—he thrived on order, structure, and clarity, which became vital as his organization faced the unpredictability of the pandemic.

Jason was used to ensuring that everything ran like clockwork, not just by overseeing how information flowed within the organization but by making sure every piece of communication aligned with the broader mission. His role was much like the backbone of the organization—keeping everything in sync so that no part worked in isolation. But the pandemic threw everything off balance. Teams were now working remotely, priorities were shifting daily, and uncertainty loomed in every department.

When the pandemic hit, the organization was suddenly thrust into chaos. As the virus spread, events were canceled, services were halted, and the nonprofit had to pivot to stay relevant and provide essential services to its community. Larger organizations with greater resources were able to adjust quickly, but Jason's nonprofit, which had always prided itself on its in-person interactions, struggled. With operations and staff scattered, communication became increasingly difficult. Some departments were out of sync, and the overall mission seemed to be drifting further away from its original intent.

Jason was facing a critical moment in his leadership. If you were in Jason's position, how would you have tackled this growing disarray? What steps would you have taken to maintain the integrity of the organization's mission while adapting to the new reality?

For Jason, the first step was to assess the gaps. His high Air Traffic Controller style naturally drew him to find the areas where the communication structure was breaking down. Before the pandemic, teams were used to regular face-to-face meetings, but now, with everyone working remotely, these vital interactions were harder to coordinate. Different departments were focusing on their own immediate needs, losing sight of the organization's larger goals.

Jason's attention to detail allowed him to see the bigger problem—the organization's communication structure had been designed for in-person operations and had not adapted to remote work. The previous methods of communication, which relied heavily on proximity, no longer worked. Without that in-person interaction, the flow of information had slowed to a crawl. Teams that once thrived on informal communication now found themselves siloed, each working in isolation.

Instead of trying to micromanage each department, Jason recognized that he needed to rebuild the entire communication system from the ground up. He took a step back and asked himself a crucial question: How do I keep everyone aligned with the organization's mission while adapting to this new environment?

Jason began by implementing a more structured, centralized communication system. He introduced daily briefings and made use of digital tools that allowed teams to stay connected in real-time. But this wasn't just about technology—it was about creating a sense of purpose. Jason made sure that every message from leadership was tied back to the organization's core mission, reminding teams why their work mattered, even if they couldn't see the immediate impact.

This is something I would advise any leader in a similar position: when communication breaks down, it's often because the messaging lacks clarity or purpose. Jason understood this instinctively, and he used his high Grounds Crew behavior style to ground the organization in its values. By constantly reinforcing the mission and vision in every piece of communication, Jason kept the non-profit's teams aligned, even when the day-to-day operations seemed chaotic.

If you were in Jason's shoes, how would you have restructured communication to maintain alignment with the organization's mission? Would you have used the same tools, or tried something different?

While Jason's Air Traffic Controller side focused on ensuring smooth operations, his high Grounds Crew style ensured that every action was rooted in the organization's deeper purpose—helping the community. One challenge Jason faced during this time was the pressure to focus solely on the immediate crisis. It would have been easy to get lost in the details of pandemic logistics, but Jason knew that to keep his team motivated, they needed to feel that their work still contributed to something bigger than just getting through the next few months.

He introduced weekly "mission meetings," where each department shared how their work was contributing to the organization's long-term goals, not just to its short-term survival. This allowed his team to maintain a sense of forward momentum and purpose. These meetings weren't about operational updates but about reminding everyone of the broader vision they were working toward, despite the chaos around them.

What would you have done to keep your team focused on long-term goals during a time when it feels like everything is falling apart?

Jason's ability to maintain focus on both the operational and emotional needs of the organization is a prime example of how a high Air Traffic Controller/Grounds Crew behavior style can be leveraged in times of crisis. His Air Traffic Controller side helped him ensure that the technical aspects of communication and operations were running smoothly, while his Grounds Crew side kept the team connected to the nonprofit's mission and values.

However, Jason wasn't immune to the pressures of the moment. There was one point, early in the pandemic, when he started to feel overwhelmed by the constant need to adjust and react to the crisis. As someone who thrived on structure, the rapid changes made him feel like the ground was constantly shifting beneath him. During this time, he had to dig deep into his own resilience, drawing from his past experiences where he learned that, even in times of chaos, maintaining a steady hand is critical.

Growing up, Jason had learned to navigate difficult situations at home. His parents went through a tough divorce when he was young, and he often found himself in the middle, trying to keep the peace. These early experiences shaped his ability to create order in the midst of disorder. It was this resilience that helped him regain his footing when the pressure of the pandemic seemed overwhelming.

Do you think your past experiences have shaped how you approach leadership in times of crisis? What strengths do you think you could draw on when things feel uncertain?

Once Jason regained his focus, he became even more determined to keep the organization moving forward. One of his biggest breakthroughs came when he realized that his team needed more than just operational clarity—they needed emotional support. While his natural inclination as an Air Traffic Controller was to keep everything running smoothly, he knew that his team was struggling with the isolation and stress of remote work. As a leader, it wasn't enough for Jason to ensure that tasks were completed on time; he needed to ensure that his team felt connected and supported.

To address this, Jason initiated weekly one-on-one check-ins with each department head, not just to talk about work but to check in on how they were doing personally. These conversations became a lifeline for his team. For many of them, the pandemic had blurred the lines between work and home life, and Jason's genuine concern for their well-being helped them stay grounded.

How would you have supported your team emotionally during a time like this? Would you have set up similar check-ins, or taken a different approach?

Jason's ability to blend operational efficiency with genuine care for his team's well-being was crucial in keeping the organization aligned and focused. His Grounds Crew nature shone through as he created a supportive environment where people felt valued not just for their work, but as individuals. And this, in turn, improved the team's performance. When people feel supported, they are more likely to stay engaged and motivated, even in difficult times.

Another important aspect of Jason's leadership during this time was his commitment to transparency. Early in the pandemic, many organizations were struggling with uncertainty, and leadership was hesitant to share too much information with staff for fear of creating panic. But Jason took a different approach. He believed that in times of crisis, transparency builds trust. He made it a point to communicate regularly with his team, even when there wasn't much new information to share.

By keeping his team informed about the decisions being made by leadership, Jason built a sense of trust and security within the organization. His team knew that, no matter what, they would be kept in the loop. This transparency also helped reduce anxiety—by addressing concerns head-on, Jason diffused some of the uncertainty that was weighing heavily on his team.

Would you have taken a similar approach to transparency, or would you have been more cautious about sharing information?

Jason's leadership during the pandemic was marked by his ability to adapt, stay focused, and keep his team aligned with the organization's broader mission. His high Air Traffic Controller/Grounds Crew behavior style gave him the tools he needed to navigate the chaos, providing both structure and emotional support. By keeping communication clear, fostering a sense of connection, and maintaining alignment with the organization's goals, Jason helped the nonprofit not just survive but thrive during one of the most challenging periods in recent history.

His story reminds us that, as leaders, our role is to be the backbone that holds the organization together. We provide the coordination and communication necessary to keep the team aligned, even when everything else feels uncertain. And while the road ahead may be unpredictable, leaders like Jason show us that with the right balance of strength, flexibility, and empathy, we can keep our organizations moving forward, no matter what challenges arise.

Shift Your Mind!

Mindset Shift 1: From Messenger to Translator of Vision

It's easy to see yourself as simply the messenger who delivers the leader's directives to teams. However, to truly drive alignment, you need to shift from being a messenger to a translator of vision. Your role is not just to pass along information but to ensure that the vision is understood and translated into actionable steps that resonate with each team.

What This Shift Means

Rather than merely relaying leadership's goals, you actively translate big-picture strategies into tangible actions. This means breaking down complex ideas into clear objectives for each department, ensuring that the message is meaningful and relevant to everyone. By adopting this mindset, you become the bridge that ensures everyone is on the same page and working toward the same vision.

To-Dos

1. Understand the unique perspectives and functions of different departments, and customize your communication to align with what's most relevant to their work.
2. Ensure teams not only know what to do but also why it matters. Connect their daily tasks to the larger organizational vision.
3. Break down the leader's broad goals into concrete, actionable steps that teams can immediately implement.

Mindset Shift 2: From Coordinator to Facilitator of Collaboration

In traditional roles, you might be focused on

coordinating activities between departments. However, shifting to a facilitator of collaboration means you're not just ensuring tasks are completed but actively fostering an environment where departments communicate and work together seamlessly. Your job becomes one of cultivating alignment and ensuring that teams aren't working in isolation.

What This Shift Means

Instead of managing tasks in silos, you create opportunities for departments to share knowledge, collaborate on joint projects, and align their efforts. This shift emphasizes the importance of collective problem-solving and shared goals, making sure every department understands how their work impacts others and contributes to the organization's success.

To-Dos

1. Facilitate regular collaboration between teams to discuss progress, challenges, and opportunities, ensuring that everyone is working together.

2. Help teams identify where their work intersects with others and foster better coordination of those interdependencies.
3. Create spaces where employees feel empowered to share ideas, provide feedback, and work collectively toward common objectives.

Mindset Shift 3: From Problem Solver to Proactive Connector

It's natural to assume the role of a problem solver when issues arise. However, as the backbone of leadership, your real strength comes from being a proactive connector—identifying potential communication gaps or coordination breakdowns before they happen. This shift allows you to keep the organization running smoothly by preventing problems, rather than reacting to them.

What This Shift Means

Rather than waiting for issues to emerge, you anticipate them by regularly monitoring communication flows and department coordination. You ensure that information moves freely across teams and that any bottlenecks are addressed early. This mindset helps you maintain alignment and keep the organization agile and responsive.

To-Dos

1. Hold periodic check-ins with teams to assess whether communication is flowing effectively and whether there are any looming challenges that need to be addressed.
2. Develop systems that alert you to potential misalignments or coordination issues before they become major problems.
3. Encourage teams to come forward with challenges early so that you can resolve issues proactively, keeping projects on track.

Owning the Shift

By shifting from messenger to translator, from coordinator to facilitator, and from problem solver to proactive connector, you enhance your role as the backbone of leadership who ensures that communication and coordination flow seamlessly. These shifts empower you to keep the organization aligned with its goals and foster a culture of collaboration and agility.

6

THE POWER OF PROBLEM SOLVING

The human backbone is remarkable in its ability to bear the weight of the entire body, especially during moments of physical strain. Whether lifting, bending, or carrying a heavy load, the backbone provides essential stability and ensures that the body remains upright and balanced. Similarly, those in key support roles handle the weight of organizational challenges and crises. These backbones of leadership provide stability, ensuring the organization remains resilient under pressure, and keep operations moving forward when things get tough.

In this chapter, we'll explore the critical problem-solving and crisis management skills required for leaders to bear this weight. We'll look at how you can handle organizational pressure, why a calm and strategic approach is crucial, and how to stabilize an organization when it faces adversity. Just as the backbone stabilizes the body during physical strain, leaders in these roles stabilize the organization, preventing it from collapsing under the weight of challenges.

Meet Sarah R., the Chief Marketing Officer (CMO) at a mid-sized marketing firm that specialized in digital advertising. Sarah had always been driven, a natural-born leader with a Pilot behavior style. Pilots are known for their decisiveness, strategic thinking, and ability to execute under pressure, but some people in her company didn't see Sarah as someone who could handle the "backbone" responsibilities of leadership. They saw direct people like Sarah as focused on their own vision, too independent to support an organization's broader needs. Sarah, however, was determined to prove them wrong.

Growing up, Sarah had always felt like she wasn't enough. As a young girl, she often compared herself to others—especially in her family, where her older siblings excelled in academics and sports. Despite her achievements, Sarah felt like she was never quite enough in her parents' eyes. They loved her, but they always seemed to focus more on her siblings' accomplishments. This sense of inadequacy followed Sarah into adulthood, driving her to constantly prove herself in every endeavor. She became laser-focused on success, striving to show that she could achieve greatness on her own terms.

This background shaped Sarah's approach to leadership. As a Pilot, she was naturally decisive, never afraid to take the lead and make bold choices. But deep down, her drive to prove herself stemmed from those early feelings of inadequacy. She was always striving to demonstrate that she had what it took to succeed—even if she didn't fully believe it herself.

At the marketing firm, things had been going well for several years. The company had grown quickly, attracting clients in tech, retail, and healthcare. But as the market became increasingly competitive, the firm started to hit roadblocks. Clients were pulling back on their marketing budgets, frustrated with the lack of measurable results. Internal teams were disjointed, each focusing on their own projects without any clear direction or alignment with the company's overall goals. It was a time of uncertainty and confusion for the organization.

If you were in Sarah's position, how would you have handled these early signs of disarray? Would you have focused on fixing the internal issues, or would you have turned your attention to the external market challenges?

Sarah knew that something needed to change. The firm's leadership was looking to her for answers, but internally, she felt the pressure building. This was a defining moment for her—one that would test whether she could truly handle the weight of the company's struggles. As a CMO, she was responsible not only for driving marketing strategies but for ensuring that her team could execute and deliver results. Her Pilot nature meant she was ready to act, but this situation required more than just bold decisions. It required stabilizing an entire organization.

The first thing Sarah did was step back to assess the root causes of the firm's challenges. While external pressures were part of the problem, Sarah quickly realized that the real issue lay within the company itself. The marketing teams were fragmented, each working in silos without a clear sense of how their efforts contributed to the larger vision. The lack of coordination was leading to missed deadlines, inconsistent messaging, and frustrated clients.

What would you have done next in Sarah's position? How would you begin to address the internal misalignment that was affecting the company's performance?

Sarah knew that her role wasn't just to oversee the marketing strategy; it was to ensure that the company's operations aligned with its goals. As the backbone of the organization's marketing efforts, Sarah needed to bring the teams together and create a unified direction. Drawing from her Pilot behavior style, she approached the situation strategically, taking swift action to correct the internal issues.

One of her first moves was to establish a communication framework that fostered better collaboration across teams. Sarah implemented regular cross-departmental meetings, ensuring that every team—whether working on digital ads, content marketing, or social media—had a clear understanding of how their work fit into the larger strategy. Ironically, she wasn't interested in micromanaging. Instead, she focused on providing clear goals, timelines, and expectations, ensuring that each team knew how their efforts contributed to the overall success of the firm.

Sarah also understood that realignment

wasn't just about processes—it was about people. The lack of communication had created friction between the teams, leading to tension and resentment. Sarah drew on her leadership skills to rebuild trust among the teams, making sure they understood that they were all working toward the same goal. She encouraged open dialogue and feedback, giving everyone a voice in the decision-making process.

In my experience, realigning an organization isn't just about setting new goals or creating new processes. It's about building relationships, fostering trust, and ensuring that every team member feels connected to the company's mission. Sarah's ability to blend her strategic mindset with relational leadership allowed her to bring the teams back together, creating a sense of unity and shared purpose.

Despite her success in realigning the teams, Sarah still felt the weight of the company's struggles. The firm's financial performance wasn't improving as quickly as she'd hoped, and she began to wonder if her efforts were enough. Her old feelings of inadequacy started to resurface—those same feelings she'd battled her entire life. She questioned whether she was truly capable of handling the pressure or whether her colleagues had been right to doubt her.

If you were in Sarah's position, how would you deal with the self-doubt that almost inevitably comes with leadership? What strategies would you use to stay focused and maintain confidence in your abilities?

Sarah knew that in order to lead effectively, she needed to address her own feelings of inadequacy head-on. She began working with a coach to develop strategies for managing her self-doubt. Together, they explored the underlying reasons for her need to constantly prove herself. Sarah learned that her past experiences had shaped her mindset, but they didn't have to define her future. By understanding where her feelings of inadequacy came from, Sarah was able to reframe her approach to leadership.

Instead of seeing every challenge as a test of

her worth, Sarah began to view challenges as opportunities for growth. She realized that being the backbone of the organization didn't mean she had to carry the weight alone. By building a strong, collaborative team and trusting in their abilities, she could share the burden while still providing the stability and guidance the company needed.

This shift in mindset allowed Sarah to approach her role with renewed confidence. She no longer felt the need to prove herself to others—instead, she focused on empowering her team to execute the company's vision. Her Pilot nature was still the driver behind her leadership, but she had learned to balance it with a more collaborative and supportive approach.

As the months went by, Sarah's efforts began to pay off. The teams were working more efficiently, delivering better results for clients, and the company's financial performance started to improve. Sarah had successfully navigated the firm through a period of internal turmoil, stabilizing the organization and setting it on a path to growth.

But Sarah's journey wasn't over. Despite the progress the firm had made, new challenges arose. A key client threatened to leave, citing dissatisfaction with the firm's performance. Sarah knew that losing this client would be a major blow to the company, both financially and reputationally. The pressure was once again on her shoulders.

In times of crisis, what would you prioritize? Would you focus on immediate damage control, or would you take a step back to assess the bigger picture?

Sarah understood that while the situation with the client was urgent, reacting impulsively could do more harm than good. She took a step back to analyze the root causes of the client's dissatisfaction. Was it an isolated incident, or was there a deeper issue with the firm's processes or client management?

Through her analysis, Sarah discovered that

the client's concerns weren't just about per-formance—they were about communica-tion. The client felt disconnected from the firm's strategy and didn't understand how their needs were being addressed. Armed with this insight, Sarah took swift action. She personally reached out to the client, acknowledging their concerns and offering a plan to improve communication and ensure that their needs were met moving forward.

Sarah's ability to maintain a calm, strategic approach under pressure was a evidence of to her growth as a leader. She had learned that being the backbone of the organization wasn't just about making bold decisions—it was about understanding the nuances of each situation and responding in a way that stabilized the company.

By addressing the client's concerns head-on and providing a clear plan for improve-ment, Sarah not only saved the account but strengthened the firm's relationship with the client. This experience reinforced Sarah's belief that the key to successful leadership lies in balance—between decisiveness and collaboration, between innovation and stability.

In the end, Sarah's Pilot behavior style wasn't a hindrance to her role as the backbone of the organization—it was an asset. Her ability to lead with confidence, make bold decisions, and think strategically allowed her to guide the company through difficult times. And while some might have doubted her ability to provide the stability the firm needed, Sarah proved that Pilots can indeed be the backbones of leadership.

Her experience is a powerful reminder that leadership is about more than just vision—it's about execution and stability. As a leader in a key support role, your ability to stay focused on the mission, adapt to challenges, and lead with both strength and vulnerability is what makes you the backbone of leadership. Just like Sarah, you have the power to stabilize your organization and guide it through even the most challenging times.

Shift Your Mind!

Mindset Shift 1: From Problem Solver to Strategic Problem Preventer

It's easy to focus on solving problems as they arise, but a true backbone of leadership shifts from simply solving problems to preventing them. Rather than waiting for issues to surface, you must proactively identify risks and vulnerabilities, ensuring that systems and processes are robust enough to prevent crises before they escalate.

What This Shift Means

This shift allows you to move from reacting to challenges to anticipating and mitigating them. You become more strategic in your approach, regularly assessing the organization's operations, communication channels, and external factors that could potentially lead to disruptions. Your proactive stance will prevent many crises before they even emerge.

To-Dos

1. Periodically evaluate all operational processes and identify weak points that could turn into larger issues.

Address them before they become urgent problems.

2. For each potential risk, create a backup plan. Ensure that teams know how to respond if things go wrong.

3. Encourage your teams to raise red flags early. Create an environment where identifying potential issues before they snowball is valued.

Mindset Shift 2: From Crisis Manager to Crisis Leader

In moments of crisis, your natural instinct may be to manage the problem and resolve it quickly. However, a shift from crisis manager to crisis leader requires you to take control not only of the problem itself but also of the emotions and morale of your team. A crisis leader maintains composure, communicates clearly, and provides a sense of direction and hope during chaos.

What This Shift Means

This shift transforms you into a leader who not only tackles the logistical aspects of the crisis but also instills confidence in the organization. As a crisis leader, you manage emotions, foster a calm atmosphere, and help teams stay focused, reducing panic and ensuring a structured response.

To-Dos

1. Keep your teams informed about the nature of the crisis and the steps being taken. Transparency builds trust and ensures that everyone is aligned.
2. Your demeanor will set the tone for the entire organization. Maintain a calm, steady presence, even in the face of uncertainty.
3. During crises, encourage teams to offer solutions and take ownership of key tasks. By involving them, you maintain momentum and ensure that the entire organization pulls together.

Mindset Shift 3: From Short-Term Fixer to Long-Term Thinker

When problems arise, it's tempting to implement quick fixes to patch things up and move on. However, shifting from a short-term fixer to a long-term thinker means you go beyond addressing the immediate crisis. You use the crisis as an opportunity to strengthen the organization and ensure it's better prepared for the future.

What This Shift Means

Instead of applying temporary fixes, you focus on identifying underlying issues and implementing solutions that will have a lasting positive impact. You prioritize long-term resilience over short-term relief, using the crisis as a learning experience to improve organizational strength.

To-Dos

1. Go beyond the surface problem to find out what caused the issue in the first place. Address these core issues to prevent recurrence.
2. Once the crisis has passed, take the time to reflect on how it was handled. What went well? What could be improved? Use this feedback to refine your strategies for the future.

3. After resolving the immediate issue, assess your processes and systems. Strengthen them to make the organization more resilient against future challenges.

Owning the Shift

By moving from reactive problem-solving to proactive prevention, from managing crises to leading through them, and from quick fixes to long-term solutions, you enhance your ability to handle the weight of leadership under pressure. These mindset shifts will ensure that you not only navigate challenges effectively but also build a stronger, more resilient organization capable of thriving even in the face of adversity.

The Power of Problem Solving

7

THE POWER OF FOSTERING GROWTH AND DEVELOPMENT

Just as the backbone supports the growth and development of the human body, the backbone of leadership plays a pivotal role in fostering organizational growth. The backbones of leadership, like you, are instrumental in nurturing talent, cultivating future leadership, and ensuring that the organization adapts and thrives in an ever-changing environment. Growth, both personal and organizational, doesn't happen by accident. It requires intentional effort from those who understand the importance of development at every level.

Lynette A., a soft-spoken, reliable introvert with a moderate Grounds Crew behavior style, had navigated her way through a series of high-level positions across various industries. She had worked in operations, finance, and strategy before settling into her current role as Vice President of Human Resources at a well-established firm. While Lynette's career had been impressive, it was marked by frequent transitions, which, in hindsight, she realized had more to do with her search for stability than a pursuit of the next best opportunity. Her upbringing in an unstable home, with parents whose attention ebbed and flowed unpredictably, had instilled in her a constant need to create order wherever she could.

Now, in her role as VP of HR, Lynette was learning that she wasn't just responsible for managing policies and people; she was responsible for fostering the growth of others. Her experience in various fields had given her a unique perspective—she understood the operational and financial aspects of the business, but her moderate Grounds Crew behavior style meant she was naturally inclined to focus on creating systems that worked quietly in the background, ensuring the stability she had craved throughout her life.

One of my observations about Lynette is that she embodies a quiet strength. She doesn't command attention in meetings or overpower others with her opinions. Instead, she listens, reflects, and offers thoughtful insights when necessary. This has worked in her favor in the role of HR, where empathy, structure, and a soft touch are essential. However, Lynette has always struggled with the idea that growth requires more than just keeping things running smoothly; it also requires intentional development of those around her.

In her first few months as VP, Lynette found herself managing a team that seemed capable but lacked initiative. They were doing their jobs but weren't pushing themselves or each other to develop further. Lynette understood that, in her role, she had to be the one to foster a culture of growth, both personally and organizationally. But as an introvert, stepping into a role that required her to actively mentor and inspire others felt foreign. She had never been the loudest voice in the room, nor had she ever sought to lead through charisma. What she did have, however, was her grounded approach to building systems that worked.

Lynette began to assess the company's HR development initiatives and saw that they were fragmented. Employees were being offered professional development courses and mentorship programs, but there was no cohesive plan linking these activities to the company's long-term goals. Without an overarching strategy, the programs were being used inconsistently, and the company wasn't seeing the benefits of a culture that truly valued growth.

She knew she had to lead the change. But how? She wasn't the type to give rousing speeches or demand immediate results. What she did know was that systems, when built correctly, could nurture growth organically. Her strategy would be quiet but deliberate—just like her.

Lynette started by creating a roadmap for professional development that tied individual growth to the organization's larger vision. She implemented structured mentorship programs, ensuring that future leaders had access to guidance, but she also focused on giving employees room to explore new skills. Rather than micromanaging, she built a framework that encouraged self-directed learning. People were allowed to take ownership of their development within clear parameters, which played to her strength of creating order without being overbearing.

One of the things I noted about Lynette's approach was how much it mirrored her own experience growing up. Just as she had learned to create structure in an unpredictable home, Lynette created an environment where her team had the support they needed to grow but also the autonomy to make their own choices. She wasn't trying to control their progress; she was laying the foundation that allowed them to thrive. This, in my view, is where her experience truly shaped her leadership style. Lynette's strength was not in pushing people, but in offering them the stability and tools they needed to push themselves.

Over time, the changes Lynette made began to show results. Employees became more engaged with their development plans, and team members who had previously seemed content to coast along started taking on more responsibility. What was interesting to me was that, despite her introverted nature, Lynette became a mentor to several younger leaders in the company. They were drawn to her calm, steady leadership style, which contrasted sharply with the more dynamic, extroverted leaders in the organization. Lynette's quiet approach to mentorship allowed these future leaders to grow at their own pace while feeling supported and guided.

But it wasn't all smooth sailing. Lynette encountered resistance, particularly from more senior members of her team who had become comfortable with the status quo. Some felt that the emphasis on personal development was unnecessary and that the company should focus more on immediate business objectives. Others didn't see the value in mentorship and resented the time it took away from their daily tasks.

Lynette faced these challenges head-on, not with confrontation, but with consistent, clear communication. She held one-on-one meetings, gently but firmly explaining how investing in people's growth would benefit the entire organization in the long run. She listened to their concerns, but she remained committed to creating a growth-oriented culture. Through her persistence and willingness to address concerns individually, she slowly gained buy-in from even the most skeptical members of her team.

My takeaway from watching Lynette is that the backbone of leadership doesn't need to be loud to be effective. Growth can be nurtured through quiet, thoughtful actions that support people in their own development.

She never tried to mold herself into a different kind of leader; instead, she leaned into her strengths, using her organizational skills and deep understanding of human behavior to foster an environment where growth could occur naturally.

As Lynette's initiatives took hold, the company began to see tangible results. Employee retention improved, engagement scores rose, and the company was able to promote from within more frequently, thanks to the development plans Lynette had put in place. What started as a soft-spoken, behind-the-scenes effort to create stability had evolved into a full-fledged cultural shift toward growth.

What would you have done if you were in Lynette's shoes? How would you have handled the resistance from more senior team members, and how would you have balanced your own leadership style with the need to push for growth?

Lynette, by creating a supportive, structured environment, exemplified what it means to be the backbone of leadership. Her approach wasn't flashy, but it was effective. She didn't need to change who she was; she simply needed to apply her natural strengths in a way that fostered growth and development across the organization. This is something all leaders in support roles can learn from—staying true to yourself while using your unique skills to cultivate an environment of growth is the key to long-term success.

Shift Your Mind!

Mindset Shift 1: From Manager to Mentor

It's easy to fall into the routine of managing tasks and ensuring that day-to-day operations run smoothly. However, to truly foster growth, you must shift from simply being a manager to becoming a mentor. Instead of focusing only on operational tasks, place greater emphasis on the personal and professional development of your team members.

What This Shift Means

This shift allows you to move beyond task

management and focus on the long-term growth of your people. As a mentor, you're not just directing work—you're guiding individuals in their career journeys, helping them discover their strengths, and encouraging them to develop new skills. This approach builds trust, engagement, and loyalty while ensuring the continuous development of talent within the organization.

To-Dos

1. Spend regular one-on-one time with team members, discussing their career aspirations and development goals.
2. Offer constructive feedback and provide them with opportunities to take on new challenges that align with their growth.
3. Encourage and facilitate their learning through mentorship, training, and development programs.

Mindset Shift 2: From Individual Success to Collective Growth

Often, leaders focus on ensuring that their own work and success are recognized. However, as the backbone of leadership, it's essential to shift your focus from individual success to collective growth. Your success is intertwined with the success of the entire team. When your team grows, learns, and thrives, the organization as a whole becomes stronger.

What This Shift Means

This mindset shift emphasizes the importance of creating opportunities for your entire team to grow, not just managing your own success. It's about investing in the potential of others and seeing their success as a reflection of your own leadership. When the collective team flourishes, the entire organization benefits, creating a ripple effect of growth and innovation.

To-Dos

1. Empower your team by delegating meaningful responsibilities that challenge them to stretch beyond their comfort zones.
2. Celebrate the successes of your team members and recognize how their individual achievements con-

tribute to the overall growth of the organization.

3. Create a culture of collaboration where team members support and learn from one another's experiences.

Mindset Shift 3: From Stability to Continuous Learning

Many leaders feel the need to maintain stability and ensure that the status quo is preserved. However, fostering growth requires a shift from prioritizing stability to embracing continuous learning. This shift encourages an environment where curiosity, innovation, and development are the norm, and employees feel safe to experiment and learn from both successes and failures.

What This Shift Means

Instead of viewing stability as the ultimate goal, this shift allows you to see continuous learning as the key to long-term success. Growth happens when employees are encouraged to seek out new knowledge, take risks, and challenge outdated practices.

As the backbone of leadership, your role is to support this culture of learning and ensure that it permeates every level of the organization.

To-Dos

1. Encourage a mindset of lifelong learning by regularly discussing new trends, ideas, and innovations with your team.
2. Promote a culture where taking calculated risks and learning from failures is seen as a valuable part of growth.
3. Provide resources and opportunities for employees to pursue continuous learning, whether through workshops, courses, or hands-on experiences.

Owning the Shift

By shifting from manager to mentor, from individual success to collective growth, and from stability to continuous learning, you set the foundation for meaningful development within your organization. These mindset shifts will help you create an environment where growth and innovation are prioritized, preparing the organization and its people for a successful and sustainable future.

8

THE POWER OF SELF CARE

We are shooting straight here. Get your regular adjustments or you will fail under the load! Do I have your attention now!

This isn't a suggestion, it's a necessity. Just as a misaligned backbone hinders movement and causes pain, neglecting your well-being will ultimately undermine your leadership. You are the backbone of your organization. Without your strength and dogged determination, the entire system struggles to stand tall and weather challenges. You drive progress, stabilize operations, and maintain focus amidst uncertainty. Your role might not always be in the spotlight, but it is undeniably critical. The organization's ability to thrive rests squarely on your shoulders.

But here's the truth: carrying that weight takes a toll. Like a backbone under constant strain, your capacity to lead depends on your own well-being. To remain aligned, balanced, and adaptable requires conscious effort. This means prioritizing self-care – physically, mentally, and emotionally. You cannot effectively support your organization if you are not strong yourself.

Some of you may already prioritize your well-being, consistently making "spinal adjustments" to maintain balance and inner strength. You are living proof of what's possible when self-care is a priority. But even if you're on the right track, don't become complacent. Just as a backbone needs ongoing adjustments to stay healthy, we all need to regularly check in with ourselves, ensuring old habits don't creep in and the pressures of leadership don't wear us down. Remain aware, vigilant, and proactive in your personal growth.

If you haven't prioritized your well-being, the time is now. Put yourself first. Even the strongest backbone needs attention. Take stock of your current state, identify areas needing adjustment, and commit to the necessary changes.

Leading effectively requires operating from a place of strength and vitality. How often have you pushed aside your own needs to meet deadlines or keep things running smoothly? While it may feel like you lack the time for self-care, the reality is that investing in your well-being is crucial for sustained, effective leadership.

Neglecting your needs leads to burnout, jeopardizing both your health and your ability to lead. To truly support your organization, prioritize self-care and find relief from constant pressure. Remember, a healthy backbone supports the whole body; a healthy leader supports the whole organization.

Past experiences – hardships, adversity, or personal challenges – can shape how we handle stress and responsibility. These experiences, whether conscious or not, influence our leadership approach. If you've faced adversity, it may be impacting how you handle your current responsibilities. But those past experiences don't define you. They are simply part of your story, and healing is possible.

Just as a backbone can heal from injury with therapy and rehabilitation, you may need to address past experiences to reach your full potential as a leader. This requires effort, but the rewards are immense. Committing to healing, whether through therapy, introspection, or support systems, strengthens your foundation for lasting success. By prioritizing personal growth, you become a healthier, more adaptable individual, both personally and professionally.

This is an ongoing process. Just as regular adjustments keep the backbone aligned, consistent self-reflection and adjustment are crucial for maintaining balance. This may involve setting boundaries, taking breaks, re-evaluating priorities, or finding healthier ways to manage stress. Regularly check in with yourself and make small changes that keep you centered and strong.

Your natural leadership style also influences your approach. Whether you thrive on structure, relationships, problem-solving, or strategic thinking, each style has its strengths. Embrace your natural tendencies, but also acknowledge areas for growth. If you excel at organization, leverage that to create efficient systems. If you're relationship-oriented, nurture those connections while maintaining operational awareness. Maximize your strengths and address any weaknesses to ensure they don't hold you back.

Successful leadership isn't about avoiding challenges, but facing them head-on with the confidence and determination to overcome them. Take control of your growth, prioritize your well-being, and handle your responsibilities with grace. Small, consistent "spinal adjustments" in your approach can make a significant difference.

This experience is about progress, not perfection. Every step you take towards greater well-being strengthens your core. You are the backbone of your organization's success. The healthier and more aligned you are, the stronger the organization becomes.

Even with significant progress, there's always room to grow. Never settle. The moment you think you have it all figured out, you stop evolving. Continuously challenge yourself, seek growth, and make the necessary adjustments. Complacency is not an option. Whether you're just beginning to prioritize your well-being or are already well on your way, there's always more to do to ensure you remain at your best.

As we conclude this chapter, make a commitment to yourself. Prioritize your well-being, not just for today, but for the long term. Regularly assess your needs, make adjustments, and do what it takes to maintain your strength and alignment.

Ask yourself: Where do I need to make adjustments? Am I prioritizing my health and well-being? What changes can I make today to be at my best, both personally and professionally?

Your health, well-being, and growth are inextricably linked to your success. Without them, the weight of your responsibilities will eventually become unbearable. But with them, you can carry that weight with strength and determination.

You are the backbone of leadership. With the right care and attention, you will be unstoppable. Take charge, prioritize your well-being, and lead your organization to victory. You've got this. Keep moving forward, keep growing, and never stop making those necessary "adjustments."

If you ever feel alone in your journey or like you need additional support, I want you to know that you don't have to do this by yourself. Sometimes even the strongest leaders need guidance, encouragement, and a reminder that they are capable of even more than they realize. If that's where you are right now, or if you simply want to take your leadership to the next level, the next section is for you. It's there to give you the tools, coaching, and support that will help you continue growing stronger and leading with even more impact.

No matter where you go from here, know that I am committed to your success. I'm here, rooting for you, and I am confident that the best is yet to come for you and your organization. Keep leading with purpose. Keep growing. And never forget that your role as the backbone of leadership is not just important—it's vital.

Shift Your Mind!

Mindset Shift 1: From Overextension to Balance

In support roles, it's easy to spread yourself too thin, constantly trying to keep everything together. You may feel responsible for handling every detail or fixing every issue that arises. But to be truly effective as the backbone of leadership, you need to shift from overextending yourself to finding balance. This means understanding your limits and ensuring you have the mental, emotional, and physical capacity to maintain your stability.

What This Shift Means

Instead of taking on everything, focus on managing your energy and finding balance in your workload. Like the backbone needs rest and recovery to stay strong, you need time to recharge and prioritize your well-being. Balance helps you remain grounded, clear-headed, and capable of offering the support others depend on.

To-Dos

1. Regularly assess your energy levels and workload to avoid burnout.
2. Set healthy boundaries to ensure you're not taking on too much.
3. Make time for activities that help you unwind and recover, so you stay strong over the long term.

Mindset Shift 2: From Self-Sacrifice to Self-Care

Being the backbone means you're often the one who supports everyone else. But it's important to shift from constantly sacrificing your needs to prioritizing self-care. The truth is, you cannot pour from an empty cup. By taking care of yourself first, you are ensuring that you have the strength to continue supporting others effectively.

What This Shift Means

Self-care doesn't mean neglecting your responsibilities—it means making sure you're in the best possible shape to handle them. It's about maintaining your physical, emotional, and mental health so you can continue being a steady presence in your organization.

To-Dos

1. Set aside regular time for activities that nourish you, such as exercise, hobbies, or simply resting.
2. Make mental health a priority by practicing thankfulness, meditation on God's Word, or other stress-relief techniques.
3. Ensure you have a support system outside of work—people who can provide encouragement and perspective.

Mindset Shift 3: From Reactive to Proactive Growth

When you're constantly focused on keeping things running, it's easy to fall into a reactive mode—only addressing issues as they come up. To truly thrive as the backbone of leadership, you need to shift toward proactive personal growth. This means consistently looking for ways to develop yourself, improve your skills, and build the phenomenal will needed for the challenges ahead.

What This Shift Means

This shift is about taking charge of your own growth. Don't wait for problems to force you to adapt—seek out opportunities for learning and self-improvement. Strengthening your skills and mindset will prepare you to face future challenges with confidence.

To-Dos
1. Regularly assess your own development needs and set personal growth goals.
2. Seek out training, coaching, or mentorship to build new skills or

perspectives.

3. Reflect on past challenges and how you've grown, using those insights to shape your future development.

Owning the Shift

It's important to remember that only you can make these mindset shifts. No one else can prioritize your well-being or growth for you. While there's a small percentage of you who are already living your best, most healed lives, don't become complacent. You can always deepen your understanding of yourself, your strengths, and how to care for yourself more effectively.

Take control of your development and prioritize yourself in the same way you prioritize the needs of your organization. By making these shifts, you'll be building a foundation that allows you to perform at your best, ensuring that you remain a strong, healthy backbone for your team and your organization—ready to bend when needed but strong enough to hold everything together.

I Am Here to Help

As aforementioned, but it bears repeating, like you, I was created to be the backbone of leadership, and since 1996, I have served in various roles where I've supported organizations, leaders, and teams to achieve their highest potential. My experience has brought me to the forefront of developing and supporting those in critical leadership positions. One of my most rewarding experiences has been serving as the lead coach for Dr. Eric Thomas (E.T. the Hip-Hop Preacher) in his acclaimed You Owe You Mastermind, where our team of elite-level success coaches have coached both aspiring and highly successful business professionals to reach even greater heights of personal, relational, spiritual, and professional success.

Through these experiences, I have developed a unique insight into what it takes to be the backbone of leadership. I understand the demands of leadership support and how vital it is to have someone focused on aligning teams, developing leadership capabilities, and ensuring that the organization is structured for long-term success.

I am available to be on retainer to assist both the backbone of leadership and primary leaders in maximizing their outcomes and workforce development. Together, we can create an environment where every leader and team member can grow, thrive, and contribute to the overall vision of the organization. My goal is to help you strengthen the core of your leadership, ensuring that your team and your organization continue to move forward with purpose and agility.

Whether you need guidance in navigating complex organizational challenges, support in cultivating the next generation of leaders, or assistance in improving your team's performance and alignment, I am here to help. By working together, we can ensure that your leadership is not only effective today but positioned for long-term success. Let's maximize your potential, enhance your workforce, and drive the outcomes you envision.

Contact me directly at: THEBACK-BONE@LDISMYCOACH.COM